"Very Good"

FREEDOM FROM WORRY

FREEDOM FROM WORRY

OVERCOMING ANXIETY WITH GOD'S LOVE PURPOSE & POWER

Read this

WRITTEN BY
G. ALLEN JACKSON

Copyright © 2011 by G. Allen Jackson

All rights reserved. No part of this publication may be reproduced in any form, except for brief quotations in reviews, without the written permission of the author.

ISBN: 978-1-61718-005-7

Scripture taken from the HOLY BIBLE, NEW INTERNATIONAL VERSION®. Copyright © 1973, 1978, 1984 Biblica. Used by permission of Zondervan. All rights reserved. The "NIV" and "New International Version" trademarks are registered in the United States Patent and Trademark Office by Biblica. Use of either trademark requires the permission of Biblica.

I dedicate this book to the community of Believers at World Outreach Church. Their passion for the Kingdom of God is a gift in my life.

Contents

Acknowledgements 9
Foreword 11

Introduction 15
Chapter 1   The Great Race 19
Chapter 2   The Weed of Worry 47
Chapter 3   The Prescription for Worry 63
Chapter 4   The Worry-Free Life 91
Chapter 5   The Trust Transfer 117

Using This Book in Classes and Groups 141
About the Author 145
To Order More Copies 148

Acknowledgements

No book emerges without cooperation. This work is no exception. Phillip Jackson has insisted that something be published; perhaps now he will relent. An exceptional staff team works hard enabling me to have space to write. My wife, Kathy, patiently endures my focus being directed at tasks. To the many who have read, reviewed and offered insights, thank you.

Foreword

When Pastor Allen Jackson approached me to write a foreword for his newest book, I gladly accepted his invitation. For twenty years I have witnessed firsthand the growth of faith in those who come to hear his teaching. I admire him for the way he helps his people find hope and follow Jesus. In just two decades, he has led World Outreach Church from two hundred in weekly worship to over eighty-five hundred—this in Murfreesboro, a mid-sized town twenty-five miles southeast of Nashville.

His style of delivery is informal, simple, and straightforward. He tells inspiring and challenging stories, and he explains the Scriptures so people—even those with no background in the Christian faith—can understand him. Week after week he says, in varying and interesting ways to his audiences: "Let me invite you to make room in your life for God, taking a step, starting today, starting small. You can do this."

We are currently living in one of the most dismaying periods of recent history. Unpleasant surprises have hammered us. We face anxiety from our troubled economy, eroding trust ~~in~~ institutions of all forms, uncertainties wherever we turn, bad news from near and far. The times we are in try our souls, whether we are humble people or part of an elite.

This point was made clear to me again recently as I listened to an audio book by a politician. The book was by a nine-time U. S. Congressman, a former presidential candidate and a current governor of Ohio, John Kasich. In his book he traces his lifelong journey of faith. As Kasich unfolded his own sense of need, I noted that the very first issue he shared had to do with the topic of the book you are now holding: worry. He described his persistent, nagging, fretful concerns, especially regarding the health of his premature twin daughters, until one of his colleagues helped him to trust that his girls were in God's watchful care. He confessed that he needed help to overcome worry. His story, that of a highly visible elected official who is certainly one of America's political elite, tells how he had received help from the words of a believing friend.

As I listened to Kasich describe his struggles, I realized anew that the message in Pastor Jackson's book would be comforting words of a believing friend to all who read them. Walking and talking with a wise and compassionate friend is a gift. Pastor Jackson is that kind of friend. We are not left alone in our afflictions and fears. Here is a path to freedom from worry.

I am glad to commend this book to you. I am confident reading it will bring God's blessing and strength into your life, as it has for mine.

Carl George
Author and Church Growth Consultant
Greenville, SC

Read Introduction

During the First World War, a French soldier carried a little slip of paper as he made his way along the bloody battlefront. Here is a translation of what that paper said:

> Of two things, one is certain. Either you are at the front, or you are behind the lines.
> If you are at the front, of two things, one is certain. Either you are exposed to danger, or you are in a safe place.
> If you are exposed to danger, of two things, one is certain. Either you are wounded, or you are not wounded.
> If you are wounded, of two things one is certain. Either you recover, or you die.
> If you recover, there is no need to worry. If you die, you can't worry.
> So why worry?

During a dark time in world history, that little bit of gallows logic caught the cynical mood of the moment.

The message, of course, was that worrying was a waste of time, because the world was out of control. There was nothing anybody could do about it.

I don't agree with this proposition, but I believe we're living in times of similar cynicism. We may not be fighting from a smoke-filled trench, but our whole world seems to have become a battlefront.

Almost a decade has passed since terrorists attacked New York City, and not a day or a news cycle passes without the concern that something could happen again. *Homeland security* used to be a redundant phrase, an idea taken for granted, rather than a key cabinet post.

The scientific community is warning us about climate change. Regardless of its true cause, we are seeing the rise of extreme weather through hurricanes, floods, and tsunamis. Nature has always reminded us of God's beautiful creation, but it increasingly becomes a picture of His wrath.

The world economy has been in critical condition since the cataclysm of autumn 2008. Crises in the banking industry and the housing industry and soaring unemployment have changed the national mood to something dark and fatalistic.

Meanwhile, we face the more mundane if universal issues of daily existence: the challenge of marriage and

INTRODUCTION

of raising a family; questions of health and wellness; the usual confrontations with loneliness, with purposelessness, with struggling spiritual faith.

As Alfred E. Neuman, the cover boy of *MAD* magazine, used to say, "What, me worry?"

Tense times; anxiety is ratcheted upward, everywhere we look. Is worry just a given for this earthly life, as it seems to be for most people we know? Or is there another way?

I believe the Bible has a bold and positive answer for that question. I invite you to join me on a journey, so that we might explore that answer together. It's an exciting journey—one that I believe can change your life forever.

At the heart of it all, worry is based on the faulty conclusion that God doesn't care, isn't powerful enough to change lives, and doesn't really know what's best for our families and us. As you read these chapters, ask God to open your heart to see the fear and anxiety you've lived with for years . . . so long that you don't even realize it's an unwelcome intruder. And ask Him to convince you that He is good, powerful, and wise. You can depend on Him in the good times and the bad, when life is coming unraveled and when it's going well. Our confidence, though, isn't based on our circumstances, but on God's character—His omniscience, omnipotence, and compassion.

As we begin, let me give you one word of advice: Be ready to run! Lace up your track shoes because this journey begins with a footrace.

CHAPTER 1

The Great Race

He foot race: a challenge as old as the human race; pure, simple competition, pushing the physical body to its limits.

As I write these words, Usain Bolt holds the honor of being the world's fastest runner. In August 2009, in the Berlin World Championships, he set a new record of 9.58 seconds in the 100-meter sprint. Just as it seems we've reached the edge of human possibility, the next generation steps—or gallops—right past it.

Few exhibitions match the tension of a race about to begin. The runners are poised, their muscles coiled, ready to explode forward in the first possible instant. The crowd is still and silent. In the moment that follows, when the starting gun sounds, these athletes will be as fully alive as it's possible to become—pumping legs, pushing frames, expending every precious ounce of human capability, all in the investment of moving from one line of chalk to another.

These runners are intent upon becoming champions. They've sacrificed weeks, months, maybe years in preparation for this single moment in time. Now they wait for the opportunity that has become their all in all. It's a picture of absolute focus.

I've never been much of a track guy. Sure, I jog (meaning "shuffle along"), but I've never felt what it's like to really rush like the wind. In the movie *Chariots of Fire*, Olympic sprinter Eric Liddell says, "I believe God made me for a purpose, but he also made me *fast*. And when I run, I feel His pleasure."

Well, God made me slow, and when I run, I feel—*really slow*. So what? I like to watch a good race, don't you? I love the intensity and the spirit of competition. Therefore, it doesn't surprise me at all that this very image was chosen by God in the inspiration of one of the greatest verses in the New Testament. A foot race is used in the book of Hebrews, written twenty centuries ago, to describe—well, the *human* race. In the heart of that book, we find this unforgettable verse:

Therefore, since we are surrounded by such a great cloud of witnesses, let us throw off everything that hinders and the sin that so easily entangles, and let us run with perseverance the race marked out for us. (Hebrews 12:1, NIV)

So much about this passage intrigues me. For example, I think of a foot race as an individual achievement. The runner reaches deep within himself, relying on his own physical resources. Yet in this verse, notice that it's all about *us* and *we*; we're in this thing together; "*we* are surrounded . . . let *us* throw off . . . let *us* run."

That togetherness is encouraging to me. And it's not just the two of us, either: we're enveloped by an immense "cloud of witnesses." What a picture this writer has painted.

I like the power and simplicity of our objectives:

1. We push away distractions.
2. We set out running.

There you have it: life reduced to its primal elements. Push away the past, reach for the future, and run like the wind!

You can see why I've always been attracted to the sheer, adrenaline-pumped challenge of Hebrews 12:1.

This one verse tells me that I'm not alone, but that God has given me *you*, and a throng of champions. It tells me that all that stuff around my feet—my sin, my failures, all those messy entanglements—can be kicked aside. And finally, it tells me to take off in a sprint for the finish line, to run and to feel God's pleasure.

What's not to like about all that? It's good news for shufflers, sprinters, and even sofa-sitters.

I have to explain another reason I have such a love for this verse. I have a degree in history but a passion for the future. That is, I'm less interested in the dry facts of a bygone era than in its distilled wisdom for a beckoning future. Yesterday is only capital to spend on tomorrow. Make sense? That's what Hebrews 12 means when it speaks of the "cloud": the past, energizing us toward the future.

Before we can run, of course, we must walk—and, in the verses just before this one, we take that walk with our host, the author. I'm speaking of Hebrews 11, where the writer has said, in so many words, "Come with me. I want you to see something about the laps that have just been completed." With that, he has opened a door, beckoned us down a hall, and taken us for a stroll through the portrait gallery of the Faith Hall of Fame.

If you visit the locker room of a college team (almost any sport), you'll find, somewhere nearby, pictures of the great athletes who have come through that program. The trophies are kept in cases where they'll inspire and motivate the current team. That's what we have in Hebrews 11 and 12—a wall for the past, and a track for the future.

Faces in the Cloud

Maybe you've read Hebrews 11 before. Like all museums, it's really a crash course in history, in this case the Old Testament. Our host now shows them all to us. We look upon them—Abraham, Noah, Joseph, Moses—and realize this isn't about historical trivia. This is about a powerful truth upon which our futures completely depend: the sheer dynamism of simple faith, the one asset capable of pleasing the Lord of Creation. Hebrews 11 is the Land of the Giants, the roll call of people who subsisted on little more than courage and a faith that was eternity-deep. They built their arks. They languished in Pharaoh's prison. They polished their faith through endless decades, watching for a promised child upon which to build a nation, or enduring though forty years of unforgiving wilderness.

As a matter of fact, there's always some kind of wilderness. The writer points to the great assembly of paintings and tells us how these pioneers made it through. "They were longing for a better country—a heavenly one. Therefore God is not ashamed to be called their God"

(Hebrews 11:16). These men and women were champions of the human spirit, living in full awareness of God's Kingdom. They set the benchmark for faith, and for stubbornly clinging to the hope of light through the reign of darkness.

Through this hallway we walk, reliving these stories until we come to the end of the corridor, arrive at that first verse of chapter 12, and catch our collective breath. For, you see, the last picture of all is a frame with a mirror inside it. The author says, "History is something that always ends in the preceding moment and waits, in the blink of an eye called the present, to see what you will do with the following one—which is the riddle of the future."

Our eyes are wide at the thought. A little bead of perspiration forms on our brow. We wouldn't know the first thing about building an ark, and we have far too many allergies to sleep on the desert floor.

"But there's good news," whispers our host. "All those people in the last corridor are going to be at your elbow. They are *your* cloud of witnesses, feeding you wisdom and motivation through their living testimonies. Now: Kick off the shackles, take this baton, and *run*."

That's the thrilling invitation of the faith-life—we are invited to be part of the adventure. God doesn't put his saints on a pedestal in order that we might feel unworthy. He doesn't say, "Stand aside for the champs, chumps. Make way for the heroes, zeroes!"

No, he has the saints standing aside for *you*. They receive their wreaths, take their place in the box seats, and chant *your name*. We may become the champions of our generation. This is an adventure in which Jesus himself says, "anyone who has faith in me will do what I have been doing. He will do even greater things than these" (John 14:12).

Do those words humble you as they do me? Yet there's no denying it. This is *our* moment in the arena, *our* time to run the race. Moses, Abraham, Noah, and the rest played their roles in the rising tide of history. Their times demanded special courage. Could it be that we are coming again to such a time?

I happen to believe that history is ticking toward a sure climax, that we are living in the last days before Christ reappears. If that is true, then God has special plans for you and me. He is calling forth unique men and women of faith to play their roles in the culmination of time itself. It is a fact that these are our days on the earth, our "last"—that is, our *only*—days. Let us run toward a God-directed future. He has marvelous things planned.

In this moment, He calls our names. He sets our course. And what does He want from us? I'll give you a hint—it's not about forming some new church committee. He's not interested in the elevation of pious behavior. Instead, His eyes move across the horizon, searching for people who feel a stirring in their soul to become world-shakers. He seeks disciples who are tired of business as usual and who are ready to make a measurable difference for the Kingdom of God.

Our Father in heaven searches patiently for those who can look into the distance and perceive, through the encroaching gloom, the finish line—and who are ready to push forward with every muscle to reach it. So here we stand. What will we choose?

The Light Run

Two clear principles emerge from Hebrews 12:1. The first is to get rid of unnecessary baggage. "Throw off everything that hinders." If you want to travel with speed, you carry as little with you as possible. For a literal race, we get it; for the human race, we are always tripping over our feet.

I read a story about a U.S. Olympic runner who was preparing to run a marathon. He went to the athletic shoe specialist and arranged to have his shoes reworked. The specialist labored through the night with the goal of finding half an ounce of unnecessary weight in each shoe and removing it. You see, the runner had done the math. Half an ounce doesn't sound like much, does it? Yet multiply that by several hundred thousand steps in the course of a marathon, and you're talking about a significant burden to carry from the starting line to the finish. The runner might not feel the difference in the first mile, maybe not even after the first five. But over the course of twenty-six miles, his agility and speed will be enhanced.

Wouldn't you love to visit a specialist and say, "Take the dead weight out of my life. Throw all the ballast overboard. I'll be back to write a check tomorrow." Yet this is just what God wants to do for you. He wants to help you unpack all the entanglements and extraneous distractions that weigh you down as you sprint along through life. What if you were to sit down today and make a list of the elements in life you could really do without—all the junk, the poor choices, the things that become obstacles between you and God?

Sometimes we think about doing that. Our eye falls upon some extraneous element of our lives, and we think, "I really shouldn't be involved in this." But the voice of rationalization says, "What's the big deal? It won't keep me from heaven—I'm completely forgiven."

That may be true, but you're going to come to a point in the race when you're exhausted, spent. It's going to feel as if you're carrying half the world on your shoulders, and it will be hard to go on. At that point, it will be impossible to complete the course that God has laid out for you. I invite you to take inventory today, and throw off everything that hinders.

What might that inventory include? Anger? Bitterness? There is no life experience that can't be overcome with the help of the Holy Spirit. Pulling it out at the root and discarding it may take a true act of will and the help of God. It may hurt a little bit at first. But you're going to feel like you're running on air when the difference sets in.

The Long Run

The second principle in Hebrews 12:1 is to run with perseverance.

You understand the idea of the marathon, right? If you're running the 100-meter dash, you explode off the starting line and give it all you've got until you cross the finish line. You go for one speed the entire race: eleven on a scale of one to ten.

But in a marathon, of course, you'll drop out very quickly if you do that. Instead there is the idea of pacing ourselves. You keep a constant margin of reserve energy, running enough to keep up but leaving enough power to call upon when you need it. At a certain point in the race, you're going to start increasing your speed toward the finish line. But you've always got to remember that it's a long race and you need to endure.

Whenever we take on something new—a diet, an exercise plan—we find great joy in coming off the starting blocks. In the analogy of Moses and the children of Israel, all of us are good travelers while the Red Sea is being parted. The question is how we're going to do during those forty years in the wilderness. Who is going to be the first to say, "Are we there yet?"

God is calling us to run with endurance. His Kingdom purposes are invested in us. Your time on earth isn't simply the waiting room for heaven—this is the life God has appointed for you right now, and it matters how you live it. It's the only shot you get. No matter what season of life you're now walking through, it's a season that won't come around again. It's the only chance you have to live for the glory of God.

You may be a high school student. That's a terrific and amazing season of life. But what if you decide it's the season of sowing wild oats? What if you settle for running through it with wild abandon, figuring that you'll give yourself to Christ when things calm down? The time will come when you'll wish you had another shot at that particular season. Our twenties, our thirties, and all the other segments of our lives have their advantages, but every age and stage has something special and unique about it—something to be won once and for all, or lost once and for all.

If you don't honor Christ as a teenager, you'll miss the spectacular blessings of that, and you'll cheat yourself out of something that can't be recovered. That particular door will close and lock securely, and you'll look at it, dream about it, and wonder about it for the rest of your years—even though you may be giving God glory in all the other seasons. Stop and honestly face the choice—my own self or a God-inspired opportunity? Would you really choose to dine on wild oats over a royal banquet with the King?

College and early adulthood have their own identities, and there are wonderful things to be done and experienced—opportunities to live for God with the freedom and strength that we enjoy during those years. Singleness is a gift, though many take it as some kind of infirmity. If you're single, God has things for you that He simply won't share with a married couple. Paul the apostle counsels you, through his letters, that if you have the chance to serve Christ in singleness, run with it! You can travel light, go places, and do things for Him. And again, you have only this one chance to get that right. Why spend that season yearning for something else? Embrace what He has given you, rather than wondering about what He has not.

As we begin to grow older, we lose certain things. We have less energy, but we have greater resources. We lose a little hair, but we gain a little wisdom. Every change in life has God's seal upon it, and a special use, carefully designed for His service *and* our joy. We must do exactly what the writer of Hebrews is telling us: Get stepping! *Now!* Can you imagine seeing ten sprinters take off, and one of them stays back at the starting line because he's not sure he's ready to run? It would look ridiculous. Hebrews 12:1 is a verse of urgency. The writer is grabbing you by the shoulders and issuing a personal invitation—to participate with Almighty God. You have been chosen! This is a race, after all.

Unfortunately, many of us are likely to roll over and go back to sleep. It's so easy for us to think that somewhere over the rainbow, we'll be able to serve God better—that it's all out front somewhere, at some misty point when God's will suddenly arrives in an engraved invitation: *Serve God right here, then back to your regular programming.* That's one of the saddest mistakes we can ever make. We serve a God of the eternal Now. We need to learn to live in the present moment, not in the past or future, because *right now* is the only point in time where He can be found.

There is a unique "hindrance" in regret. Often we glance backwards and are filled with remorse. If you missed opportunities and now are left with the bitterness of the realization, remember—we serve a God of restoration. "What if" and "if only" are tyrants. Do not allow them to rule your life.

Eyes on the Prize

In the next verse, the writer gives us a third critical principle:

Let us fix our eyes on Jesus, the author and perfecter of our faith. (Hebrews 12:2)

The big idea, of course, is running with perseverance, one of the toughest things to do. How do we make a marriage stand the test of time? How do we keep ourselves excited about our daily work, when it's the same thing day after day? The secret of perseverance is purpose. For Christians, that means focusing on the one in whose honor this race is run. When our minds are set on Him, that changes the way we see marriage. It makes a difference in daily work that otherwise would be drudgery. We embrace each day, with all it brings, to live for God's glory.

Do you ever see Olympic sprinters gazing into the crowd as they run the 100-meter dash? No, their eyes are fixed on the end line like lasers. When you run the race of your life, fix your eyes on Christ. Don't be distracted by the scenery. After all, what is a Christian? He or she is a "Christ follower." That's the literal meaning of the word. We aren't running with no direction in mind. And that lane isn't always smooth. It's not a "weather-proof" surface, like the state-of-the-art tracks used by today's sprinters. Jesus tells us that following Him leads everywhere He goes, and that includes the cross—the first principle we learn when we fix our eyes on Jesus.

Jesus endured the cross.

Let's face facts, and face them squarely. To embrace Christ means to embrace the cross. Sometimes Christianity is misunderstood. It is imagined to be a path to a struggle-free life, a way forward with no challenges or disappointments. In truth, everyone's lives unfold with unwanted events and circumstances. Christ-followers live with the awareness that God walks with us, that we are not alone or powerless no matter how dark the season.

Jesus rejected the shame.

We come to the second thing that Jesus did for us—one we seldom take into consideration.

Have you ever thought about the awful power of shame? We're not talking about guilt here, but genuine shame. Guilt speaks to what you've done; shame speaks to who you are—the very core of your identity. It says, *You're worthless. You mess up everything you do! Your life is defined by godless choices, and there's nothing you'll ever be able to do about it.*

Shame is deep, devastating—paralyzing. It also paints with a very broad brush, pulling in everyone you know, all in order to reinforce itself. *You've been a bad friend for him; you've really let her down; you don't deserve people like them.*

You know what? it says. *You deserve everything you're getting.*

On the cross, Jesus bore our shame and the rejection that accompanies it. He was rejected that we may be accepted. No matter how horrible our life choices, God does not reject us. He is not ashamed of us.

Think for a moment about all that Jesus endured. He was cruelly rejected by people He was trying to help—religious leaders, scholars, even his hometown friends. In the end the soldiers mocked Him, strangers spat on Him, and the crowds cried "crucify him." Jesus was alone, beaten physically and stripped of everything. He endured the cross and its shame so that you and I might be accepted.

Shame is not something God intends for any human being. Contempt is nowhere to be found in the Great Physician's medicine bag.

Whatever you may have done, the power and forgiveness of God allow you to lay down the burden of your personal history and walk a shame-free path. No one enters God's temple by the back door; all of us are equal heirs to the Kingdom.

Jesus overcame opposition.
Consider him who endured such opposition from sinful men, so that you will not grow weary and lose heart (Hebrews 12:3).

How do you stand silent before accusation, face the bloodthirsty mob, take the beating, carry the cross, then die upon it, and dare to call yourself an overcomer? He prevailed over unfair, unrelenting opposition, and so can you.

Life is not fair. Somehow we continue to be surprised at this reality. We do our best and we receive less. We go out of our way to demonstrate kindness, only to be repaid with rejection. In the midst of these very real life stations, it is important to remember that even Jesus faced opposition.

At first it seems odd, the idea of God's son being opposed. He healed someone and was accused of "helping on the wrong day of the week." He opened blind eyes and they said He did it with demonic assistance. It seemed that no matter how great of a kindness Jesus demonstrated, His adversaries found fault.

If it happened to God's son, it is safe to assume that we might face similar opposition. Jesus was not distracted or discouraged. He kept on demonstrating God's love whenever He was given the opportunity.

When Scripture warns us "not to grow weary" it is a sure bet that we will have seasons when weariness seems like an appropriate option. Some days you just get tired of doing the right thing. It is in those seasons that we make the most progress, when we persevere. That is Jesus' lesson. He endured the cross and was richly rewarded. God will be just as faithful in our lives.

When you are weary and think no one notices the burden you carry and the suffering you endure, remember our lives are ultimately in the hands of "the one who judges justly." God is our vindication. He is our rewarder. Your investments in God's Kingdom will never be overlooked or diminished.

Do not grow weary.

On the back end of verse 3, we find this wonderful clause: "so that you will not grow weary and lose heart." I gain heart just from reading these words, don't you?

Now it begins to come together. We've talked about crucifixion, of voluntarily following someone to a painful place. We've discussed shame and opposition, yet you've been led to believe that this book is about anxiety. The connection now begins to come clear.

Jesus doesn't lead us into these hard things because He wants us to suffer; He leads us in that He might lead us through. We are going to arrive at a beautiful destination, and the only road there includes difficulty. But Jesus urges us not to give in to weariness, not to let go of our faith in a heavenly ending.

Not only is this an encouragement, however; it's also a warning. The fact is that it's not just a good choice to avoid giving up—it's the only choice. When the Scriptures warn us about something, it's very wise to take note.

We live in a sinful world, a darkened place in which the stars seem to be flickering out, one by one. The blackness around us can get inside us and darken our spirits, make us lose heart. Have you ever gone deep into the country, into a totally dark night when there was no moon and unseen clouds blocked every star—then turned on your flashlight or lit a match? The more overwhelming the darkness, the more powerful and shocking is the light—even the smallest light—that suddenly flares up to challenge it. Light does not flee from darkness—precisely the opposite. The whole world, the vast universe, can be in the grip of darkness, but a single candle will chase the blackness.

When I grow weary, I think about that principle. It's not a matter of the volume of the gloom that surrounds me, but the insistence of the light that inhabits me. There is no darkness powerful enough to snuff out the Light of the World who lives in my heart.

I remember some lines from a song I learned as a child.

This little light of mine,
I'm gonna let it shine...

Don't give in to weariness. Don't lose heart. If you don't protect your flame, you will become lost in that black expanse. What God begins in you, He will complete.

These are the conditions of the race we run, as laid before us in Hebrews 12. They tell us that everything depends upon who Jesus is and what He has done for us. He has run a perfect race, and He beckons us to fix our eyes on Him and run with perseverance.

As we've already observed, we're running a megamarathon rather than a sprint. Any long-distance runner will tell you that the mind, not the legs, determines the success or failure of the racer. So it is our task to have the mind of Christ, and we look to Him to discover what that mind should be like. We come to our primary text from His very mouth.

At the end of each chapter, you'll find some questions designed for personal reflection and group discussion. Take some time to think deeply about the truths you've discovered in the chapter.

Questions

1. Hebrews 12:1 compares our lives to a race. What advice does scripture give us for effectively completing our course?

2. List some of the obstacles faced by the people listed in Hebrews 11.

3. What obstacles do you find in your path that threaten to keep you from completing God's course for your life?

4. Are there things you need to "throw off" to run more effectively (sin, weariness, shame, etc)?

Prayer: "Read"

Heavenly Father, today I choose to follow the path you have marked for me—may your will be done in my life. I need your help. Where I am weary, renew my strength. When I am distracted, by your grace redirect my attention. Holy Spirit, help me to recognize anything that hinders my progress. In Jesus' name, amen.

Notes

Notes

Notes

Notes

CHAPTER 2

"The Weed of Worry"

The Sermon on the Mount is the centerpiece of Jesus' public teaching. At the center of that presentation are Jesus' insights regarding worry.

> *Therefore I tell you, do not worry about your life, what you will eat or drink; or about your body, what you will wear. Is not life more important than food, and the body more important than clothes? Look at the birds of the air; they do not sow or reap or store away in barns, and yet your heavenly Father feeds them. Are you not much more valuable than they? Who of you by worrying can add a single hour to his life? (Matthew 6:25–27)*

The command is clear: *Do not worry.* Jesus then uses the example of clothing. The lilies are gorgeous, worthy of Solomon in all his splendor, and it had nothing to do with toil or tears—merely the expectation that God will do what He has always done.

Does He love us any less than the birds, the trees, or any of the creations that He maintains? Therefore *do not worry.* Simply "seek first his kingdom and his righteousness, and all these things will be given to you as well. Therefore do not worry about tomorrow, for tomorrow will worry about itself" (Matthew 6:33–34).

Any number of wise theologians might spend their lives pondering these words; philosophers can take them apart and reassemble them. But in the end, we are struck by how simple and straightforward the prescription of Jesus really is. In our day, we would summarize them in a manner something like this:

Get a grip! If God can tend every garden on the planet, He can surely handle you.

This thought becomes one of the foundational ideas of the New Testament. Here is how Paul phrases it:

Do not be anxious about anything, but in everything, by prayer and petition, with thanksgiving, present your requests to God. And the peace of God, which transcends all understanding, will guard your hearts and your minds in Christ Jesus. (Philippians 4:6–7)

Jesus says, do not worry about clothing, money, or food. Paul says, do not be anxious about anything. What do *you* say?

By the way, the same Greek word is translated as *worry* for Jesus and *anxious* for Paul. In the end, our Lord and our apostle are saying exactly the same thing. Worry is not helpful. Whenever you give in to it, you have lost a battle that God has placed you in the position to win.

We can say it in even more basic terms. God commands us not to worry, and therefore anxiety is disobedience. It is an act of rebellion against heaven. We have a hard time understanding that, because worry is something we keep between our ears. We believe it does no one any harm, including ourselves (doctors know better). Sin, on the other hand, is something we think of in terms of visible activity and of victims.

Surely it's just hyperbole, an exaggeration for emphasis, to take something as benign and ordinary as worry and call it sin, right? Wrong. Jesus says not to commit adultery; He also says not to worry. Neither is part of the perfect plan of God, and that places them firmly in the "to be avoided" category.

We might also object that at least we're in good company when we give in to anxiety. Some pretty advanced Christians worry, right? Read through Christian history or look at the annals of church leadership today and you'll discover that worry challenges everyone.

Worry can even be packaged as a kind of benevolent concern, can't it? "God has placed this on my heart," we say. Sometimes we present pious prayer requests that ultimately amount to the baptism of old-fashioned worry. We stand and share with the group how worried we are, and in the eyes of people, we seem more godly rather than sinful. People comfort us by praying aloud or perhaps worrying with us. We can have a good round of prayer requests and multiply the worry in the room! That's certainly not what Paul has in mind, when he tells us to pray as an *alternative* to anxiety.

When I find the words "do not" in my Bible, I make a note of it. If God tells me not to do it, I have that on the highest authority. There are many things I *wish* He would put on the "do not" list—wearing a tie, cutting the grass, going to the dentist. I can't find those things forbidden by Scripture, but I can find the clear and simple idea that I should no more worry than kill, steal, or lie.

It's Written in the Signs

What can we see in the direction not to worry? It's pretty clear to us that nothing good comes from it. As Jesus says, we can't add a day to our lives in that way. As doctors say, we can subtract a good many days by being constitutional worriers.

But why? Is God actively, intentionally punishing people for worrying—making bad things happen to them as the penalty? No. Worry fills our lives with "empty calories." We become bloated with our concerns and fears. At the same time, worry chokes out the opportunity to experience the moment we are in. Worry borrows trouble from tomorrow and allows it to cast shadows on today. That habit is simply not helpful. When God says "do not," He is not limiting our lives; He is identifying the best pathway forward.

But we don't like warnings or regulations, and we tend to turn our wrath on the messenger. This is why people say the Ten Commandments are nothing but a bunch of negative "Thou Shalt Nots." I don't see it as "negative" to tell people not to murder me or steal my possessions or spouse—do you? And I don't think the packaging of my food is simply spoiling the fun when it advises me not to eat the contents after a certain date. Some call it negative, I call it life-saving.

We've come across two traffic signs, one placed by Jesus and one by Paul, that say, *Do not worry*. We know that should we stubbornly ignore the sign and drive on, there will be no point in blaming God for what happens. Just read the signs.

Choked by Weeds

The meaning of the word *worry* has changed through the centuries. In Old English, it meant "to strangle"—literally, to choke the life from something. As the centuries passed, and language entered the phase we know as Middle English, the word had slightly shifted from strangling to simply grabbing by the throat. I once read about a wolf "worrying" a lamb. This actually referred to the wolf using its great jaw to grab the lamb by the throat.

As language entered the modern world, we came to better understand the world of thought and emotions. The word *worry* came to have its present association with anxiety or concern. But the thing itself has never changed. Worry is a strangler. It will sneak into your life, grab you by the jugular, and choke the health out of you.

Worry may seem like something you do in the privacy of your own mind, but its effects are not confined there. It has real-world consequences.

Jesus made another interesting reference to the effect of worry. He told a story about a man who went out to sow seeds. The seeds fell on four different kinds of ground and grew—or failed to grow—depending on the soil in each case. In three of the four cases, the plants failed. The analogy, of course, is to what causes people's lives to flourish or flounder. The seeds that fall among thorns, Jesus said, remind us of how "the worries of this life . . . come in and choke the word, making it unfruitful" (Mark 4:19).

There we have it: choking; strangling. That's what worry will do to your life. It becomes an invisible wall between you and God. No matter how often you attend church, join home Bible study groups, and participate in mission projects, the sharp thorns of worry can grow up to throttle your spiritual life. We remember that writer in Hebrews telling us to "throw off everything that hinders and the sin that so easily entangles." You can't run a good hundred-yard dash through a thorn field. Nor can you pursue life's best when you're knee-deep in anxiety. It will choke out your faith. It will contaminate your rational thinking and darken every emotion. It will even take a toll on your physical health.

It's important to me that we see this insidious activity for what it really is, because too many of us keep it in a neat drawer marked "acceptable sin." Do you have one of those drawers? Things like so-called "white lies" are kept in it. I've never understood the coloring of sins; I had thought they only came in black. But there are sins we wink at, such as certain lies, or church gossip disguised as godly concern, or well-intentioned worry.

There is another drawer marked "serious sin." To some extent, society tells us which sins to take seriously, and we follow that signal rather than embracing a God-perspective. I once helped a woman who had been raised in Vietnam with little exposure to Christianity. She had experienced a series of jarring tragedies and was left decimated, physically and emotionally. A concerned neighbor began to show her kindness. Through simple expressions of concern, she was introduced to Jesus. One day she asked me a simple question: "Why does the Bible say that adultery is wrong?" She was reconciling her worldview with her growing understanding of God.

As Christ-followers, we are forced to wrestle with the awkwardness of reconciling our worldview with God's perspective. Often we have condoned what God warns is destructive. Our culture has taught us to take everything with grave seriousness and to believe that worrying is a sign of a responsible person.

Worry is not a victimless crime. It can disrupt your life, and it can hurt those around you. It will steal from you the very best that God has prepared for your life. Move worry to the top drawer of sin. As a matter of fact, all you need is one drawer.

Questions

1. In Matthew 6:25-27, Jesus cautions against worry in 3 specific categories, what are they?

2. What are the areas you worry about most frequently?

3. Paul provides an alternative to worry in Philippians 4:6-7. What does he suggest we do?

4. As an alternative to anxiety, list 3 or 4 things for which you are thankful today.

Prayer:
Heavenly Father, I entrust myself to your care. I purposefully lay aside each point of anxiety and fear. Thank you that your angels are watching over my life. May your peace fill my heart. You are my refuge and my strength. In Jesus' name, amen.

Notes

Notes

Notes

Notes

CHAPTER 3

The Prescription for Worry

God doesn't want you to spend your life mired in anxiety and consumed with nagging thoughts about "what if," "if only," and "what might have been." He offers us a strategy for finding and dwelling in "the peace of God, which transcends all understanding." Well-meaning friends often give us advice that's easy and breezy. "Stop worrying," they say, "and lay your problems at the foot of the cross. Just have faith!" That sounds wonderful, but we need more than platitudes and clever phrases. We need practical strategies to help us arrive at a better destination. Here's a solid series of steps you can take to confront the problem of worry.

Decide What Matters Most

Strangely enough, I find that most people have never sat down to enumerate precisely what is important to them. What is the most important value in your life? How would you describe your life mission? Which things are essential, and which are expendable?

It's nothing you can do in three minutes; perhaps that's why so many of us are vague on the subject of priorities. We need to sharpen our attack in daily life—to know exactly what we intend to accomplish each day, what heads the list, and what items we should throw off lest they entangle us.

It may not be as easy as you think. For example, not every obstruction is an evil thing to be cast aside. Some distractions are actually legitimate tasks. Think about the time when Jesus was at the home of His friends, the sisters Mary and Martha. The former sat at Jesus' feet, listening worshipfully to all that He said. The latter was consumed by hostess chores. Both sisters were doing things we would classify as important; indeed, in our culture, we would praise the hostess with the strong work ethic; as for the "dreamer," well, we wouldn't be so sure about her. But Jesus told the frazzled Martha, "You are worried and upset about many things, but only one thing is needed. Mary has chosen what is better" (Luke 10:41-42).

Martha wasn't the only one in danger of missing Jesus' visit. In Jerusalem, the religious establishment was so complex, so preoccupied, that it missed the miracle of His teaching, His healing, His whole miraculous presence. They were worried and upset about many things when only one thing was worthy of their attention—a thing before their very noses that they tragically missed. We are all hardwired differently. There are many Marthas among us, but there are a few Marys too. Each one of us must sort through our priorities and discover what is essential—how to reorder life by the day, the month, and the year. The Mary-types, who major on books, prayer, and daydreaming, need a reminder to take care of their bodies, which are holy temples, and to live a tidy and organized life. The Martha-types, precise and regimented, need to stop and feed their minds and souls occasionally. The most focused among us are surprised, in the midst of busy-ness, to find ourselves missing God opportunities—we are so ingrained with movement that slowing down seems wrong or inappropriate.

But that vignette from the life of Jesus is about more than housework and holiness. It's about every subtle temptation we face to elevate some good thing above its station. Consider marriage, a God-blessed covenant between man and woman. At its best, we can become so enmeshed in this wonderful gift that the union takes the place of God. It was never designed to do that.

Work is a sacred thing, imprinted in our DNA. When we find the type of work God made us to do, that's a glorious thing. But many people become consumed in that work, and God vanishes behind the Tower of Babel that is constituted by an ambitious career.

What about church? Could it possibly be that we turn worship inside out, so that we find ourselves centered on the institution rather than the God who is its true focus?

All of these are issues of anxiety that actually begin in priority. Worry has a curious way of taking secondary issues and allowing them to obscure the significance of the moment. We miss the chance to laugh with a friend because we are worried about "more important matters." As we understand our priorities of the moment, we find freedom from the tyranny of worry.

Recognize the Deception of Wealth

I've often observed that there are two places where our true priorities are revealed: our checkbook and our calendar. Those are extensions of ourselves, precise and public markers revealing what matters to us. We are true to ourselves in the way we spend our money and our time, the two great currencies of today.

The Apostle Paul addresses the issue with great insight. He cautions us not to put our hope in financial resources but to focus our trust in God, "who richly provides us with everything for our enjoyment" (I Timothy 6:17).

This is not an envious condemnation of someone who has accumulated more than I have. It is an invitation to redirect our trust. It is a sobering reminder that wealth is deceptive. Often we imagine our possessions will protect us and bring us contentment. Joy, fulfillment, and peace cannot be purchased; they emerge from a personal relationship with Jesus of Nazareth. Do not be content with religious activity; it will never satisfy. A personal faith in a living Christ brings hope to any life.

We're quick to say, "Sure, I get that. I need to be less materialistic and more spiritual." The problem is that the choice has a sharper edge than that. "No one can serve two masters," He says. "You cannot serve both God and Money" (Matthew 6:24). At this very point, in the next verse, He commands us not to worry about all these things. It is a hard-line choice not to worry—the choice of God above the superficial things of this life. To set our eyes on Him is to see worry melt away.

As a matter of fact, Jesus spends a great deal of time on this subject in the Sermon on the Mount. He warns us against the deception of material comfort, telling us that wherever our treasure (priority) is, our heart will follow. In Matthew 6:19, He has urged us not to store up wealth on earth, susceptible to rust and robbery. Instead, we should seek the things of God, "and all these things will be given to you as well."

It's simple to hear but difficult to embrace, because the deception of wealth is so powerful. We come to believe that the things we have are the things we earned. The Bible never criticizes the earning of wealth, as long as we do it with honesty and integrity. What God's Word is interested in is the effect on our hearts. "Sure, I have a house and a car. I worked hard for them. I earned everything I have!"

The truth, as Jesus states, is that all good gifts are from above. They can be gone at any moment. Job, the Old Testament sufferer, said that he came naked into the world, and that he would leave in the same way. Yes, we work, and we are paid accordingly. But there are many people in the world, often God-loving people, who work even harder and have nothing to show for it but blisters and aching muscles. Where are their "earnings"? When God sent you into the world, you might just as easily have been born along the Amazon Basin in a village with

---

Note: There is absolutely nothing wrong with money or abundance. Financial resources provide options for life. There are many circumstances which are improved with a healthy cash flow. However, money is deceptive. It causes us to believe it can provide things—protection and security—which it cannot. Only God can secure our lives.

no electricity and worked practically from the womb to the tomb simply to survive.

We need a reality check when it comes to wealth. A good dose of humility is essential equipment, because wealth can easily bring with it a dose of arrogance. The Bible assures us that work is good and wealth is good—as long as we are clear-eyed about what is in our hands. The clear-eyed believer gives God thanks for everything and can be the master of his possessions without being mastered by them. The greatest worriers in the world are not people who need money, but people who have too much of it.

Learn to Pray

Another remedy for worry is prayer. It may be obvious, but that makes it no less true. Make prayer an absolute priority.

Most pastors will tell you that one of the most common admissions they hear is that people aren't sure how to go about praying. It's one of the subjects we discuss the most and do the least. Yet there's no great mystery to prayer; the Scriptures are rather definite on how to go about it.

Let's look again at Paul's passage dealing with worry. In Philippians 4, he urges us to be anxious for nothing and to be in prayer for everything. Then he packs a marvelous and detailed strategy for that into just a few words. "But in everything, by prayer and petition, with thanksgiving, present your requests to God" (v. 6). Then, he promises, God's incredible peace, something far beyond our understanding, will "guard your hearts and your minds in Christ Jesus" (v. 7).

These verses are almost mathematical in their deliberation. First, what are the values? "Anything" and "Everything." What can't we be anxious about? Anything. What do we pray about? Everything. Have you ever heard two children competing to call a higher number? "I call a hundred!" "I call a thousand!" Pretty soon one of them will "call infinity," because there's no possible answer to that one. The other kid will say something like, "infinity times infinity," but we know the game is over.

Paul is calling infinity here. Worry about nothing, because you can't worry about less than that. Pray about everything, because you can't pray for more things than that.

Having defined his values, he offers a kind of equation. Letting our requests be made known to God = (prayer + petition) × thanksgiving. That means talking to God and asking God multiplied by gratitude to God.

In Paul's math, what does it all add up to? We are turning our hearts and minds—our thinking and our feeling—toward God. We are letting heaven inside us, and it's interesting how that works. Heaven expands to fill the space available (we're doing physics now). It leaves no room for nagging worries. Anxiety is pushed right out by our concentration on laying our needs before the Lord and simultaneously being thankful for what He will do.

I would say, "You do the math," but Paul has already worked out the equation for us. The sum, he concludes, is the "peace of God, which transcends all understanding" (peace > understanding). He's basically calling infinity again. God's peace is too powerful to be measured, at least in human terms. We can't fathom its power, particularly because it is not peace in the absence of turmoil, but in its very midst.

Please know that this is not to say that prayer is your "get out of jail free card" for every problem; the problem itself may not be going anywhere. What changes is your approach to it. Those around us wonder how we can experience true peace in a situation that would make them so anxious. This transcends their understanding.

Paul, you see, writes these words as he sits under house arrest by the Romans. He knows that the time will come for his execution. He also knows there are a million things he'd like to be out doing, particularly for a young, far-flung church in turmoil. But he has a peace that comes from heaven itself.

This is Noah having a picnic in his ark during a flood of global proportions; Jesus wondering why the disciples are so terrified by the storm that is rocking the boat; David hiding for years in caves while Saul hunts him down to kill him; Joseph rotting away in an Egyptian prison; Abraham waiting another decade for that promised child to come; Job losing everything he had other than a nagging wife and annoying "friends." Each one of these people had a promise from God, and each one must have had moments of doubt.

These men represented a stillness in the eye of the storm; a calm that is actually reinforced by turmoil rather than shattered by it.

If you're worried, apply Paul's equation. Talk to God. Ask God, and be thankful every moment for all that He has done for you. You'll find these thoughts will fill your mind and leave no room for anxiety.

Think of prayer as a coin with two sides. Let's look at prayer more closely.

Talking

If prayer is a two-sided coin, one side reads, "Hello, God, it's me."

Speak to God as you would anyone else, just as if He were in bodily form, sitting in the room with you. I have cultivated a personal habit of awakening each morning and saying, "Lord, thank you for another day." That might seem like a bland statement to you—no poetic splendor, no profound devotional thought in those words. The important point is that I'm practicing the presence of God; I'm reaffirming that He is beside me from the first moment of my consciousness that morning, and opening the channels of communication.

I love to pray while taking a walk. I can look at everything I pass—a tree, a cloud, a dog, another person—and recognize some aspect of His artistry, and I'll have something new to thank Him for. I'll also talk to Him as I would a friend or family member, if they were taking the walk with me; I'll go into what's on my mind, what's happened that day, what I'm anticipating for tomorrow.

These are the little things that make your relationship with God truly a relationship. We throw around that word, but how can we use it honestly if we never talk to the person we're supposedly in a relationship with? You can't have a relationship with anyone on earth without direct communication. Why would it be any different with God?

Listening

The other side of the coin is listening. In any conversation, we must do some talking as well as some listening. This latter is, of course, the part that causes most people to stumble. "What if I listen—and don't hear anything?" they say. "That will hurt my faith!"

I would suggest that not listening will do even more damage, because in that case you've decided you're not going to hear anything. In that situation, you certainly won't.

People ask me, "How do I listen to God? Do I hear words? Is it like a tingling or some physical sensation?"

In my forty years as a believer, I have made a discipline of listening to God. In a handful of occasions, God has spoken to me in a way I would describe as audible. Usually this happened because I was so dense that I wasn't going to pick up on any other kind of signal. He loves us and He knows there are times when He has to do what is necessary to get our attention.

Most of the time, He speaks into the context of my life in such a way that I can recognize His voice. I might be reading my Bible or listening to a song. I might even be listening to another person, and I'll recognize that God has something to say to me through my friend. On a walk or during some other activity, I might build an impression of something He is saying to me. I've learned to listen for His voice throughout the day. This is a basic part of growing as a believer.

I think about friends of mine who are avid hunters. I'll ride with them down the road, and I'm amazed at their ability to see animals I never would have noticed.

They're simply attuned to looking for them. The fact is that we are more prone to find something when we're looking for it. It's the same way with hearing God's voice. Prayer is not a five-minute daily exercise, but a way of life that will allow you to keep in step with the Spirit of God and to be far more aware of what He wants to say to you.

How about prayer together—say, husband and wife? Yes, that's an essential. If you're not doing it in your home, it's time to start. It can be as simple as grabbing your spouse's hand in the morning and saying, "God, thank You for my wonderful partner. Amen." Before you can mess anything up, you've gotten that day and that relationship off on the perfect track. Try doing that several consecutive days and watch how it enhances your love.

We are hesitant to pray with people who live under the same roof, because they know us so well. They've seen us at our worst. But that's all the more reason to pray together. This isn't about creating a spiritual façade. It's about connecting our home to God.

Know that God Is Aware

You also want to cultivate a mindset of resting in the knowledge that God is watching—and not just watching, but engaged with the details of your life. I heard about a mother who walked her kindergarten child to school every day. When he started first grade, she felt it was time that he could walk the short distance himself. She took him along one last time, pointed out all the things to be careful about, and made him aware of the safety patrol.

On the big morning, he walked to school with great trepidation. It was scary at first! But he made it to the crosswalk, he made it across the street with the nice safety lady's help, and he got all the way to his desk. He was one proud little boy.

What he didn't know was that his mother was with him every step. She was just a little behind and off to the side, making sure she wasn't seen but always there in case of emergency. She wanted him to grow, but there was no way she wasn't going to be watching out for him on that first morning.

We don't know that God is there watching us, but He is—always. When we know that He is never far away, we don't worry.

We have a wonderful and powerful doctrine in our faith. It's called the Incarnation—God putting on skin and becoming one of us, identifying with everything that is part of the human experience. "For we do not have a high priest who is unable to sympathize with our weaknesses, but we have one who has been tempted in every way, just as we are—yet was without sin" (Hebrews 4:15). Christ took on every temptation and showed us how to confront it. When we think about His example, we are encouraged; we don't worry.

The next verse in Hebrews invites us to go before God's throne confidently, "so that we may receive mercy and find grace to help us in our time of need" (v. 16). Do you realize what that verse does not say? It doesn't say to wait until you've become very humble, very pious, and have conquered all your problems; then put on your best clothes and approach the throne of God.

No, come into His presence in your time of need! Come when the perspiration rims your forehead, when you're weary and heavy laden, when you don't know what to do. Come when you feel anxious. We are invited to approach God in the seasons of our greatest failures. Even though He has commanded us not to worry, it's going to happen. And God is eager to enfold us in His arms and offer these two wonderful gifts of mercy and grace.

Know, then, that God is aware; that He wants to do something about your anxiety; and that He has everything you need to face it. He put on flesh once, so He has been there and done that. He knows every emotion that courses through you. If you think you're worried, imagine what Jesus felt as He prayed in the garden, knowing the nails would soon cut through His wrists and ankles. Yet when Peter attacked those who came to arrest Him, Jesus told the fisherman to sheath his sword; legions of angels were at Christ's disposal, but He pushed aside the fear and chose to trust God. The root of worry is fear. We fear what we cannot control. Trust is the antidote. He accepted all these things so that you could approach Him with confidence. He let the devil take Him by the throat so that you wouldn't have to let worry do that to you.

He knows how you feel. Cry out to Him! Go into His presence and lay it all before Him. He may not remove the problem, because there's a good chance He's more interested in your growth than your immediate comfort—and growth often comes through adversity. It is a privilege when we are presented a circumstance that enables us to grow in faith. It is a doorway to an entirely new future. Instead of being overwhelmed with anxiety and fear, rejoice that God would choose you for such an opportunity.

Give the Problem to God

Peter, the man with the sword, became stronger and wiser after those events. Here is what he told us to do with our worries: "Cast all your anxiety on him because he cares for you" (1 Peter 5:7).

Imagine that you're stumbling down the road with a huge sack over your shoulder. It holds every item of anxiety in your emotional inventory. Some of them are large; some are small. Many are squirming in that sack; some smell terrible, and it's all that you can do to walk under the weight of this burden. Then a stranger walks up beside you. He says, "Excuse me, but I'm a good bit larger than you. I can handle that bag. Would you allow me to carry it for you?"

You do so, and the two of you walk along, enjoying wonderful conversation together. It's still your bag. You're not delegating the things in there that are your issues and responsibilities. You'll need to sit down at various times, sort them out, and make some decisions. But you don't need to carry them on your weary shoulders all the time. Peter tells us to cast all our cares upon Him.

The Scriptures never tell us to abandon our responsibilities. If you're a parent with a rebellious child, the solution is not to simply "blow it off" and think of other things. You must deal wisely and lovingly with the issues at hand. But it's a lot easier to do when you're guided by the rational mind of Christ rather than the irrational worry of anxiety—when Christ carries your burdens.

Why is this so difficult for some of us? Isn't it odd that we can trust God with the greater thing—our eternal destination—but have trouble trusting Him with the relatively smaller issues of this life? If He is faithful for one, He must be faithful for the other. The great challenge of our lives is to learn, increment by increment, to trust Him implicitly, down to the finer points of daily living. Then we can begin to find victory over the worried mind.

Don't Worry About What God Is Doing in Others' Lives

There's a fascinating conversation at the very end of the gospels.

In the final chapter of John's account, Jesus has returned. They're at the beach, fishing and then cooking breakfast as the sun comes up. For the disciples, all is right with the world once more—except something that is gnawing at Peter.

Jesus has that famous conversation with the fisherman in which He restores His friend to fellowship after the disciple had betrayed Him in the moment of crisis. Jesus gently tells Peter that he, too, will someday walk the road that leads to a cross. "You will stretch out your hands, and someone else will dress you and lead you where you do not want to go" (John 21:18). Then he looks at Peter and says, "Follow me!"

Peter seems to accept this, as devastating a revelation as it is. But he turns and glances at that other most intimate disciple of Jesus—John, who is following behind them. "Lord, what about him?" he asks.

Jesus replies, "If I want him to remain alive until I return, what is that to you?" And He repeats, "You must follow me." (v. 22).

As the book's author, John adds that this statement caused a rumor that John would not die, but he points out that this isn't exactly what Jesus said. It was a kind of theoretical statement. *What if John—or some other friend—never dies at all until I come again, Peter? What difference does that make in your mission? Two words, my friend: Follow me.*

In a matter of a few minutes and a couple of bites of grilled fish, Peter has covered a lot of ground. Just minutes ago, he felt unworthy to be a disciple; now he is "helping" Jesus manage His leadership.

It's a bit like those days when you're sitting in church and recognize that God is inviting you to change—then you find yourself looking at that fellow in the next row, the one who irritates you. *Lord, what about him? I sure hope he's hearing the words of this sermon. You and I know he needs it, Lord.*

Don't we have enough worries of our own to confront, without expanding our concerns to God's choices for others? Believe me, trusting God for His best in your life is task enough. Keep your gaze fixed on the soul inside you rather than the one beside you.

Learn to Live One Day at a Time

Don't you love these words of Jesus? "Therefore do not worry about tomorrow, for tomorrow will worry about itself. Each day has enough trouble of its own" (Matthew 6:34).

Every coach knows that ultimate sports cliché, "We'll play 'em one game at a time." Jesus is telling us to live with that philosophy. Each day has just the right number of problems. Time is God's way of prioritizing our assignments; we are to live in the present and deal only with the day He has given us.

Again, please don't understand this as the Bible's license for you to be derelict in your duties and irresponsible. God has a plan, and there's plenty for you to do. But His plan is always planted firmly in the Now. That's where we live, not in the past, not in the future. We are eternal creatures, and one day we will live in an existence not marked by passing moments. But for this chapter, we live one day, one hour, one minute at a time. What would happen if we placed our focus on making it the most godly moment possible?

I'll give you one clue about what would happen—you would be liberated from anxiety. How much time do we spend worrying about the future? It's good to plan for it; it's bad to beat up on ourselves inwardly over it. Maturity is learning to maximize this day for the glory of God, being aware of just what He wants us to do, then going and doing it. The more active we are in serving Him, the more we will experience His incredible peace.

Questions

1. How does the pursuit of wealth, pleasure, and possessions inflame worry and crush our sense of contentment?

2. As we pray about our concerns, why is thanksgiving so important? What happens when we pray but forget to thank God for all the things He has done for us?

3. Does "casting our anxiety on God" mean that we sit passively and wait for Him to work things out for us? Why or why not? What is God's part, and what is our part in the resolution?

4. Comparing our life circumstances with others can foster frustration or fuel our determination. Sometimes we feel others are receiving more favorable treatment than we are. At other times we recognize the suffering of others which we have avoided. Can you think of an example of each response from your own experience?

5. When is it appropriate to think about the future, and in what cases is it distracting and destructive?

Prayer:
Heavenly Father, I rejoice today because you are my provider. I am your child and you are aware of all my needs. I thank you that you are Lord over my circumstances, your grace and power are sufficient to meet all my concerns. Today I give you all my anxiety and frustration. I choose your peace. Holy Spirit, help me to be content, to trust and to yield to Almighty God. I choose to turn my thoughts toward the majestic Kingdom of my Lord and rest in His provision, in Jesus' name, amen.

Notes

Notes

Notes

Notes

CHAPTER 4

The Worry-Free Life

At this point we've advanced on certain fronts in our discussion of worry. We learned a perspective Jesus brings to the problem. We began with the example He set of enduring the cross, rejecting shame, and overcoming opposition. He met the problem of sin head-on rather than in-head, through worrying about it.

We've learned that it's actually His command, not His suggestion, that we reject the option of worrying about life. It's like any other godly command, forbidden because of what it does, strangling us from the inside out, choking us at our point of connection to the things of God. When Jesus dealt with the most basic ideas of daily living in the Sermon on the Mount, He said, "Do not worry."

None of us want to worry, particularly after we reflect on all these terrible effects on our lives. All of us know that God has better things in mind, and so we begin to apply God's remedy for worry. We take a fresh look at our priorities, beginning to put things in their proper place. That in itself is freeing to the mind. We learn better and deeper ways to pray. We know that if we can simply be better listeners to the voice of God, we won't feel the solitude and frustration that elevates our problems. We lay our cares before Him, we ignore what He is doing with others, and we set out to live one day at a time.

Yet something's still missing. As we think about life ahead, we wonder if even these nuggets of heavenly advice are enough. We are still weak, even if they are strong. Life means a daily barrage of new issues. Sure, Jesus says not to worry, but we wonder how much strength it will take to avoid it.

In this chapter we're going to discuss the "big picture" issues that will help us formulate a lifelong approach to confronting long-term anxiety. There are powerful truths we need to understand, and powerful provisions to help us put them into action. Let's explore the key perspectives that help us quickly unload worry and anxiety.

Trust Trumps Fear

You'll remember how Jesus approaches this subject in Matthew 6. In verse 25, He tells us not to worry "about your life, what you will eat or drink; or about your body, what you will wear." He turns to nature—animals, then plants—to illustrate why worrying makes no sense from a heavenly perspective.

We can imagine sitting on the hillside, listening to the greatest sermon ever preached. We watch as the Master gestures at the clouds above. "Look at the birds of the air," He says. He makes the point that birds are notoriously poor farmers. They're great at flying, and they make wonderful singers. But birds make no attempt to sow or reap or put aside a food supply in the barn. How do they eat? God feeds them through His providence in nature. He has built a beautiful system, a circle of life that provides even these small creatures with all their needs. That's His point about food.

Then we watch as Jesus points to a patch of lilies gently swaying in the breeze on a nearby field. This is His argument on the topic of clothing (or, we might add, possessions of any kind with which we "clothe" our lives). The beauty of the lilies can't be improved upon.

Jesus points out that those who are so caught up in acquiring—food or things—haven't recognized the greater invitation, "But seek first his kingdom and his righteousness, and all these things will be given to you as well" (Matthew 6:33). Things, in other words, are standard equipment in life. God is going to provide them, and when we worry, one of two things is happening: 1) we have been distracted from a God agenda, or 2) we have abandoned trust and embraced fear. His Kingdom is the place of security. His agenda is the thing that calls for our mental energy.

This means that we need to entrust ourselves to His care. We don't abandon responsibility for life—we redirect our trust. How can we do that? It requires living on earth while thinking from a heavenly perspective. This is the beginning of wisdom. It's no promise, of course, that we will never worry again; on the day that you're absolutely and totally free of worry, you'll be in another world, not this one. But a God's-eye-view means that you live with the mind of Christ, and anxiety is momentary rather than pervasive.

For example, many people have lost their jobs in recent times. There's no way that's going to happen without us worrying a little bit. If it hasn't happened to you, perhaps you've been anxious about a friend or family member who is coping with unemployment in a jobless economy.

I recognize that I struggle between two perspectives. I truly believe that God will provide for me as surely as He does the birds of the air. I believe there will be shelter and clothing as surely as the tiny, airborne seeds of the flowers will find a place to take root.

Yet, there are seasons when I struggle mightily with life's setbacks. I battle worry and fear, and a God perspective seems far away.

The effort to work through the struggle brings strength to our lives. I believe God is sovereign and loving, and I accept that He works in all things for our good. To reject that is to believe this life is random, there is no safety net, and we're on our own. I would be worried, too, if I believed that.

Jesus invites us to try on a new perspective. He has one that allows our thoughts and emotions to soar above the tumult. Confidence is founded in a God who is interested in my best.

Do you not know? Have you not heard?
The LORD *is the everlasting God, the Creator of the*
   ends of the earth.
He will not grow tired or weary, and his under-
   standing no one can fathom.
He gives strength to the weary and increases the
   power of the weak.
Even youths grow tired and weary, and young men
   stumble and fall;
but those who hope in the LORD *will renew their*
   strength.

*They will soar on wings like eagles;
they will run and not grow weary,
they will walk and not be faint.
(Isaiah 40:28–31)*

What can we learn about the heavenly perspective from that passage?
1. God is involved in our lives, and He never takes a break.
2. He pays special attention to strugglers.
3. Struggling does not make me weak. It makes me normal.
4. Heaven-minded people get well faster.
5. God will restore what has been lost.
6. With God's help, I will finish well.

Jesus and the Small Picture

Jesus, then, gave us a new way to look at old problems. If we can learn to gaze around us through heaven's bifocals, we'll see much clearer, and we're going to like what we see.

But let's also pay some attention to what He did *not* say. For example, He refused to get into details when it came to the problems of this world.

We're always quick enough to raise those questions. If I saw you and noticed that you were weighted down with anxiety, and I said, "Be encouraged—remember God loves you and will care for you," you might reply, "But you don't know what I'm going through." And you would give me the details, say, of how you lost your job, how it was a specialized field, and how there are absolutely no other jobs available.

If I noticed that you had a lot of anger, and it was directed at the fellow who fired you, I would say, "Be forgiving. That's how God wants us to live." You might reply, "But you don't know what kind of person I'm talking about." And again, you would get into those specifics. We are very reactive to circumstances—small-picture thinkers more often than big-picture.

Jesus didn't say a word about the economy, the housing crisis, or the state of our lending institutions. He never said a word about global climate change, the immigration problem, or rival nations acquiring nuclear capability. We like to talk about what Jesus said about this or that issue, but in fact He has left us with silence on many specifics. Instead, He gave us position papers on . . . lilies of the field; birds of the air.

If we'd been given a bit of Q and A time with the Master, I doubt we would have asked any questions about those two subjects. We want specifics!

Why? Jesus understood the true nature of daily anxiety. He had little concern for international politics or issues of global controversy. He knew that the circumstances of personal, day-to-day life are the things that consume us. As I stand in church on Sunday morning and look across the rows of faces just before worship, I wonder what's going on inside all those heads. I'd guess that few of them are meditating on international politics or ecology. More likely they're thinking about jobs, about families, and about the challenges of health.

We worry about the things that touch us within the boundaries of our daily experience. That's how it is now, and it was the same way during the events of Matthew's gospel. Jesus looked out on His own listeners and knew what was inside those heads. "Don't worry about your next meal," He said. "Don't worry about the clothing on your backs," which was all most of them owned. He was looking at the "small picture," speaking to them right where they lived, and He speaks to us in the same way. The message is so simple: "God will take care of you."

I once read an observation of American culture, and its truth chilled me. The writer said that it was difficult to engage Americans in true concern over global issues, even issues of terrorism. The reason is that Americans have the ability to medicate the tension away with a trip to the mall. Even in the midst of a great financial crisis, most people I know still have the affluence to "cocoon" at home with their widescreen televisions and DVD collection. We lead such comfortable lives; it's simple to make ourselves believe there aren't people starving, dying of illnesses, even being tortured for their faith, in other parts of the world.

The problem isn't that we're Americans, but that we're human. We live in the moment, in the immediate. Jesus understands this, and He speaks to us in that context. We worry about our family relationships, about next week's medical examination, about whether we can hold on to this job. Maybe it's true that we're self-absorbed, but just the same, Jesus meets us where we are. He wants us to know that God loves us and will care for our needs.

He also knows that once we take our eyes off ourselves and look to God, the problem of self-absorption will be remedied. In the beginning, we will look to Him simply for His providence. That's okay—children are selfish, wanting to know only what's in it for them. But trusting children grow into adults. They begin to find that the same God who feeds us and clothes us also provides incredible fellowship and guidance. It turns out that when they come to His throne and offer themselves as "living sacrifices," that's the moment when they actually find themselves. He says, "Whoever loses his life for my sake will find it" (Matthew 10:39).

It's among the more beautiful paradoxes of the Kingdom.

A Remarkable Invitation

Jesus is inviting us to such a remarkable life. Few people realize just what our experience in this world could be if we would only accept in full the offer He is making. We need not be slaves to fear and anxiety over our needs. As a matter of fact, He tells us in verse 32 of chapter six that "the pagans run after all these things." In other words, those who trust God have clear heads; those who don't must hurry and scurry in a life of uncertainty.

We need to remember that there were two kinds of people in Jesus' audience. One was the Jewish people, God's Covenant nation, who had received the direct revelation of the Lord of the universe. The other was—everyone else. Jesus, of course, came so that this wall of distinction would topple, and everyone might have the direct revelation of God. But at the time of the Sermon, there were people who had the Law and people who didn't. The latter couldn't be blamed for worry, because they knew no better. They "run after all these things"—they spend their time chasing *stuff*. For Jesus, the chasing of stuff is pagan—godless.

The invitation of Jesus, on the other hand, is life on a much higher level. "Seek first his kingdom and his righteousness, and all these things will be given to you as well" (Matthew 6:33).

It works this way:

Chase *stuff*, and you'll never stop running, nor experience the peace of God.

Chase the peace of God, and you end up with both.

As C. S. Lewis put it, "Aim at heaven and you will get earth thrown in. Aim at earth and you get neither."

Sadly, this has proven to be a difficult lesson to learn. We get the whole thing backwards, thinking we need to take care of business first, then settle down and become a Christ-follower. "I hear you, Lord," we say. "And I intend to follow you—really I do! I just need to get my ducks in a row first. I need my career to be set up and running. I need to get my family in place, get the right house, get a little older . . ."

That time never comes. We seek the things rather than the One who gives them, and we find that we never stop running.

George Müller took Jesus at His Word. Müller was a man who lived totally by prayer. The burden of his heart was orphanages, and he was a visionary about providing shelter for as many homeless children as possible. In time, he was housing and feeding two thousand boys and girls in five different buildings. (When he began, England had accommodations for no more than three thousand orphans in the whole country.) What's remarkable about Müller is this: He decided from the beginning he would do it without the ordinary grind of fund-raising and promotion. He spent no time courting donors, putting letters in the mail, or guest-preaching about his mission so that people would support it. He simply prayed and did what the birds did: expected God to provide food. Müller kept a prayer log that recorded ten thousand answered prayers, some of them absolutely miraculous.

In one case, he came to bedtime knowing he had no food for breakfast the next day. The children would go hungry unless God intervened. The next morning there was a knock at the door, and it was a man with a meat wagon that had broken down outside. "All this meat is going to spoil," he said. "Do you by chance have any use for a whole lot of meat?"

So it went for George Müller. He minimized worry, even with the incredible responsibility of feeding so many young mouths. He knew two things. First, he was walking in the will of God. Second, God had promised to provide.

I can tell you this about my life. Almost every point of paralyzing anxiety has come when I've been distracted away from the things of God and become invested in me, myself, and I—my plan, my agenda, my wants and demands. All I could see was things, even if they were worthy things, things that God wanted. You can worry for the best of reasons, but worry is still a sin.

What would your life be like today if you put the horse before the cart? What if you began to seek the Kingdom of God rather than be consumed by the anxieties of living? What if you learned to trust the horse to run, rather than expending your energy trying to push the cart with your own strength?

Life changes when God's priorities come to the top. Isn't it time to stop making your God-life *a* priority, and make it *the* priority? It's the invitation of a lifetime from Jesus Christ. You have nothing at all to lose, and everything in the world to gain.

A Separate Peace

We've seen the life to which Jesus is inviting us. But how do we get there? God has made a provision; otherwise we'd never get off the starting blocks.

Let's visit Jesus during another teaching session. This one, however, feels very different. In the first one, He was in the great outdoors, teaching beneath the sky to a crowd. In this case, he is in a darkened upstairs room, with only His closest friends in attendance. Then, He was speaking about the basics for everyday living; now, He is revealing some of the deepest mysteries of His relationship with the Father.

It is the evening of the Last Supper. Jesus knows the terrible fate that is reserved for Him in the next few hours, but He is pushing back the worry. As He speaks about leaving this world, the disciples are the ones who are plagued by anxiety. What will happen? Where will they go? Who will lead them? Jesus gives them remarkable news:

> *But the Counselor, the Holy Spirit, whom the Father will send in my name, will teach you all things and will remind you of everything I have said to you. Peace I leave with you; my peace I give you. I do not give to you as the world gives. Do not let your hearts be troubled and do not be afraid. (John 14:26–27)*

The disciples try to make sense of this news. Jesus, it seems, is shipping out. But He is sending a counselor—an advisor—to take His place. A "personal trainer" will remind the disciples of all that Jesus has taught. But there is another legacy. "Peace I leave with you," Jesus says, and not only peace but "My peace." He comes again to the subject of worrying as He asks the disciples not to let their hearts be troubled.

How is it that we, the followers of Jesus Christ, can ever be consumed by worry when we have a personal counselor who is resident in our hearts? How can any of us be developing ulcers when the peace of Christ Himself is our gift?

What we would like, of course, is the peace that means absence of conflict. But this is not part of the offer. The road to resurrection leads through Calvary. There would be nothing at all remarkable about the peace of Christ if it flourished in tranquility. Who doesn't offer peace that works when life is peaceful?

No, what He offers us is a peace that is strong during the storm, that goes with us to the cross, and that has nothing whatsoever to do with the ebb and flow of circumstance. It is a separate peace, one that life cannot take away.

We could say many things about Jesus, but not that His life was peaceful. It began with His parents fleeing into Egypt to keep Him from being slain by a tyrant. In the first days of His ministry, He had to leave town because of an angry mob. Religious leaders taunted and accused Him wherever He went, and Jerusalem, His least safe destination in the world, was precisely where He headed. *Turbulent* is a much better word for His life, yet His legacy is peace. So never even begin to think that He wouldn't understand what you're going through. He faced the worst that humanity can offer without becoming a victim of anxiety, and He provided us a model for peace while the storm rages.

He understood that life challenges everyone. Anyone who follows God as a way to comfort and easy happiness is misguided. Jesus never came to remove us from the problems of the world, but to enable us to be triumphant in the midst of it. His peace makes that possible.

"Do not let your hearts be troubled," He says to His disciples right in the shadow of the cross, just around the moment when His betrayer stealthily slips from the room. "Peace I leave with you," He says, as His executioners sharpen the nails that will soon push through His hands and feet. Before departing for prayer and an appointment with the guards, He spends these moments comforting and reassuring His worried friends. They don't understand these words about a counselor coming to take His place. They can't realize how radically different they'll be after the day of Pentecost, when that Holy Spirit arrives to spark a fire that will rage across the Mediterranean world and ultimately every inhabited continent.

They are about to discover the power of the Spirit-filled life.

The Power of the Spirit

As Christ-followers, we have the Holy Spirit with us. The Spirit of God will guide us and remind us of a God perspective. He is also a comforter, someone who will challenge our anxieties with faith and hope.

This is the very key to the worry-free life. We need not labor to achieve some peaceful state of consciousness on our own. He is a Spirit of peace, and we cannot fail to experience that peace ourselves, if we will only be aware of His presence. My advice to you: Do not resist the work of the Holy Spirit.

Our faith is based on who God is, not what we have done. Its foundation is the crucifixion and resurrection of Jesus Christ, who died for our sins and rose to conquer death. Because He paid the price for our sins, we can stand in God's presence freely forgiven, pure and whole as Christ Himself. This is what the Spirit reminds us; this is why we have peace. God the Father has given us His laws, and Christ has given us His teaching. Then He died for us two thousand years ago. But the Spirit is with us in the moment. His reach is unlimited by time or space.

"My peace I give you," Jesus said. That's a gift that keeps giving, because the Holy Spirit imparts it to us every day.

When something difficult happens at work, the Holy Spirit is there to put it all in perspective. He gently nudges into the realm of our awareness Romans 8:28, which we've hopefully lodged somewhere in our memories. That verse reminds us that in all things, including this day at the office, God is working for our good. When anxiety would threaten to make us dissatisfied at home, around our family, the Holy Spirit offers peace. He reminds us that we can love as God loves, and that these people are precious even though they are not perfect.

Don't fall into the trap of being afraid of the Holy Spirit, as if He were going to take over your body and make you a pious robot. He will never embarrass or humiliate you. He will not immediately walk you over to the harbor and put you on a boat for distant ports as a missionary. He will make possible the ultimate version of yourself—the person God wants you to be, which is the future of all futures.

Keep in step with the Spirit. That's when life truly begins to be exciting.

Questions

1. Think of a time when you trusted God in a difficult situation. How did trust trump fear in your life? How does it help you to remember times when you trusted God?

2. What are some of the "little things" that can consume our thoughts with anxiety? Are they really little, or are they genuinely significant? Explain your answer.

3. What did C. S. Lewis mean when he wrote, "Aim at heaven and you will get earth thrown in. Aim at earth and you get neither"? What does it mean in your life to "seek Jesus first"?

4. Most people think of "peace" as the complete absence of difficulties. Is this what Jesus promised? If not, how would you describe His offer of peace?

5. What is the Holy Spirit's role in helping us trust God with our difficulties?

6. Ask God to give you wisdom about the kind of peace He offers you, and trust Him to lead you clearly in a particular problem you're facing.

Prayer:
Heavenly Father, my desire is to learn to trust you, to put my hope in you. Help me to lay down the fear and concern and to be more aware of your presence. Thank you for caring for me. Thank you for accepting me, inconsistencies and all. Holy Spirit, guide my steps, may my heart be open to your direction, in Jesus' name, amen.

Notes

Notes

Notes

Notes

CHAPTER 5

The Trust Transfer

Think about a time when you've felt anxious. What other emotions were you experiencing? Did you also feel confused, frustrated, and alone? Perhaps what you really needed, or particularly appreciated, was a good friend—someone to serve as a sounding board, someone to help you brainstorm about what to do, and, invariably, to assure you that things weren't quite as bad as they might seem.

This is the radical difference the Holy Spirit makes in our lives. Paul writes the following words to an anxious younger friend: "For God has not given us a spirit of fear, but of power and of love and of a sound mind" (2 Timothy 1:7).

The context here is fear; some translations render this word as *timidity*. Aren't these the emotions we feel when we're anxious? Fear is intense worry, and it makes us anything but bold. We become timid and hesitant to act. Paul is telling Timothy that when he gives in to fear and backs off from the situations he's facing, something is wrong.

God wants us to know that the Holy Spirit is incompatible with rampant fear. The Spirit brings us three bold, assertive qualities that have everything to do with knowing God's peace:

Power. This doesn't mean physical power, but a special kind—the energy and dynamic of God's presence through the Holy Spirit.

Love. This doesn't mean a sappy emotion or a romantic feeling, but the unconditional, unselfish love that can come only from God.

A Sound Mind. This is best translated as self-discipline, which would give you the ability to stay focused and rational rather than giving in to worry.

Worry puts us on the sidelines of life. We are fearful, timid, and tortured by "what-ifs." What if I lose my job? What if something terrible happens to my child? Worry is the very opposite of a sound mind, because it causes us to think irrationally, and it freezes us into inaction. The Holy Spirit, on the other hand, brings us the power to act, the love we need for others during a challenge, and the self-discipline to be cool under fire.

No, you couldn't respond in this way on your own. The Holy Spirit is your counselor, your advocate sent so that you may live as Christ did in this world. The Greek word is *paraclete*, which means "one who is called alongside" to help you. When you begin to worry, your first thought should be, "I'm not alone."

Therapists, by the way, tell us that the worst thing for anxiety is solitude. They advise us to seek out friends when we're plagued by worries. By ourselves, we magnify the situation. The next time you find yourself worrying, you need to seek out a friend—but not just any friend. You don't have to take a step or dial a number or send a text message. It's strengthening to know that you will never spend a moment of the rest of your life alone or helpless. You have an advocate with you, called alongside for your benefit. He is filled with love and wisdom and power. This fact alone should dissipate many of life's worries.

A God-Directed Life

Long-term freedom from worry, then, is about learning to live a God-directed life. As we do that, we also begin to transfer our trust, very gradually, from our own control to the sovereignty of God.

Think of how we grow as human beings. As infants, we are totally dependent upon our parents for every need. The job of the good parent is to slowly but surely teach us how to gain increasing independence. By the time we've weathered adolescence and entered early adulthood, we should be grappling with the challenges of caring for ourselves and making sound and ethical judgments about how to live.

Most of us enjoy being "on our own." We believe we are captains of our own fate, masters of our destiny. The invitation of Christ, however, is the final step in true human development. He invites us to move from normal autonomy to a spiritual dependence upon God. We are still adults who know how to care for ourselves. But on the inside, something is very different. We don't believe we are captains of our own fate at all, but children of God's Kingdom. We know He is in control, and we seek to follow and please Him.

God will never dominate your life or refuse you the privilege of choosing direction. He extends to each of us an invitation to follow. One of the mysteries of the Kingdom of God is that Almighty God allows each of us to choose our pathway.

Learning to Let Go

If you had a key ring that represented various issues in your life, how many of them could you say you had taken off the ring and handed over to God?

Let's think about what happens when we can't bring ourselves to do it. It's easier, at least for the moment, to hold back. It's normal human nature to want to be in control of as many elements of life as possible. But how's that working out for you? What's your personal ratio of worry-time versus time of contentment? Yes, it's always within your power to clutch that particular key (perhaps you have one in mind right now) a little tighter. As our fists stubbornly close over the thing, other things close over us: Anxiety. Fear. Worry. Together, they will strangle any sense of peace we might have.

Do you really feel a legitimate sense of autonomy in this life—that is, are you holding to the proposition that you know better than God what will work in your life? When we put the idea forward in such frank terms, of course, it sounds ludicrous. But isn't that the true nature of the issue?

To find life, selfishness must diminish—true freedom is found only in true dependence. Until we embrace that truth, I'm afraid we must live in a cloud of worry and fear. Your goal should be to come to that day when you can say, "I live this life as an ambassador of another world—a heavenly kingdom. I trust God implicitly, no matter how large or small the issue might be. When I confront an uncertain situation, I will face it honestly and take responsibility for handling it well. But it will not become an item of worry, because God, who is so much greater than I am in every conceivable way, is the one who owns me, this problem, and this world."

That's what the life of peace looks like. The individual transfer of each issue may be a little painful at first, but the peace at the other end is more than worth it. It's also true that the inner battle will never completely disappear; there will always be that impulse to close our fists over the issues of our lives, to horde control over this or that item, so that the self-focused life—and its resulting anxiety—stages a rally to regain control. Meanwhile, the quiet voice of the Spirit whispers to our inner soul, reminding us of the words of Christ: "Come to me, all you who are weary and burdened, and I will give you rest. Take my yoke upon you and learn from me, for I am gentle and humble in heart, and you will find rest for your souls" (Matthew 11:28-29).

It's a daily decision—I have discovered this after many years of struggle. Each morning I must face the new day with the resolve that God will be present in the midst of my day. For every micro-decision, the old voice inside says, "Are you sure? Come on, don't you want to own this one for yourself?"

I must then stand firm and nail one more matter to the cross. After all, my strength comes from what Jesus accomplished on my behalf. With each right decision, each item that I lay before the throne, I am transferring my trust to God. The applause of heaven can almost be heard, the Spirit lends His voice of encouragement, and the next time I will find just a little more strength to make the right decision. Meanwhile, my mind is beginning to experience true freedom from anxiety.

This is my creed: "'Not by might nor by power, but by my Spirit,' says the LORD Almighty" (Zechariah 4:6). Believe me, my human nature never tires of the idea of might and power, of taking the world by the horns and making everything all about me. But I'm learning that it doesn't work; my responses alone are inadequate for the God-sized invitations that are before me, and it leads only to a life of fear and worry.

The devil tempted Jesus with thoughts of might and power in the wilderness:

Why not use your miraculous abilities to change these stones to bread, rather than cultivate the discipline of closeness to God through fasting?

Why not make a big public sensation by leaping off the high point of the temple, with legions of angels coming to catch you in mid-air?

Jesus, with all His power, chose the way of obedience and the Spirit. Can I do any less? It's not as if I can make anything in life work by taking hold of it myself, given my severely limited wisdom and human flaws of judgment. I want to take off in so many directions, in obedience to so many impulses. How, then? What can I do to make this trust transfer begin to happen in my life? I believe there are two vital steps that each of us must take. I know of no other path.

Trust Everything to God

There's no more basic consideration I can lay before you. You must acknowledge the Lordship of Christ in your life. Have you done that? Think before you answer.

I believe there are many people who have spoken the right words, but are still jealously clutching their personal autonomy. They will not give up the throne of life. To be a Christ-follower is to yield to the authority of the Lord of lords. To allow His priorities to begin to influence my priorities, His passions to direct my passions.

Simply sitting in church won't accomplish that. Attending a Bible study, or four of them, won't do it for you. Neither does it matter how devout your parents were. This is a soul negotiation; no one is at the table but you and Christ, and you must venture into the deepest part of your heart to sign over yourself, your very heart—to transfer the trust to God.

And what have you given up? Your false sense of control; your sins; your fear and your worry. Jesus says, "Come to me when you're weary and heavy-laden. Give me those things that weigh you down, and I will give you a brand new life in exchange—one whose yoke is easy and whose burden is light."

Does He have a deal for you!

Welcome the Holy Spirit

Once you're "all in," you need to understand about the place of the Holy Spirit in your life. As we've seen, He is the one who makes it all happen. What an incredible relief to know that you're not on your own in this new way of living life.

You need not invite the Holy Spirit, because He came in at the moment you accepted Christ. What you do need to do is listen to Him, cooperate with Him, and learn to walk in His power. In all those little struggles in which you transfer trust to God, He is the agent who takes charge of these things, handling the details.

Therefore it's important not simply to know He is there, but to welcome Him. How do you handle a new neighbor where you live? Some people watch the moving van from behind the blinds, then perhaps nod curtly when the two of you walk to the mailbox at the same time; others are quick to ring the doorbell with a fresh plate of brownies. The latter means, "I found out you've arrived, and I want you to know you are welcome." From that moment, you are going to be friends. Don't watch the Spirit from behind the blinds. Welcome Him.

Welcome the Holy Spirit into your life and give Him your full cooperation. He provides the secret of life lived to the full, and you need to cultivate a strong and intimate relationship with Him as you would any human friend.

Recognize Your Vulnerability

The last aspect of this transfer has to do with recognizing your vulnerability. It's very important that we grasp this reality check. You can understand every word of this book and begin the great adventure of trusting everything to God. No matter how excited and determined you are, you're going to "leak."

We follow God with the best of intentions, but the worries still creep in somehow. When this happens, don't give up. Don't decide that this whole pursuit has been a lie. The best highways have potholes, don't they? An interstate can have all kinds of obstructions but still lead where you're wanting to go.

You need to recognize your vulnerability and know that each little failure is an encouragement to trust God more implicitly. There is a problem we have in the

Church; we create these façades of pious perfection. Again, we have the best of reasons—we want to provide a model for others. We love God and we want to show what He's done in our lives. And frankly, it's embarrassing when we spring the leaks and everyone sees. Yet those are the opportunities for us to be honest with one another, to support and encourage each other, and to learn together how to do it right next time.

We men in particular want the confident swagger of mythical figures—John Wayne or some other hero. Transparency is for sissies, right? We want to be the gunslinger who has no points of weakness, no fear of the flying bullets. The problem is that Christ calls us to honest humility rather than the mask of invulnerability.

Proverbs 4:23 counsels: "Above all else, guard your heart, for it is the wellspring of life." The heart is vulnerable, and an accumulation of little hurts can harden it. A collection of bad influences can turn it astray. Remember what Paul told us: Prayer allows the peace of God to guard our hearts and mind in Christ Jesus.

The world is difficult. Challenges, tests, surprises, and temptations hurtle toward us at the speed of life. God is there for us, but keeping our hearts connected to Him takes patient, daily maintenance and repeated refocusing. The challenge of life, they say, is that it's so *daily*. The disciples saw incredible miracles—the blind made to see, the masses given food—and still they doubted. The storm came, and even with Jesus beside them, they were afraid.

We, too, will face many storms with the Spirit of God living within us. The extent to which we stay connected will determine the success with which we will control our fear and prevail over the challenges. So let's guard our hearts and set forth with Christ on the great adventure.

The Promise: God Will Take Care of You

Most people today have heard the name of J. C. Penney, the great retailer who founded a business empire. He led a fascinating life, building his business to a high level only to lose it, then rebuilding a greater one from scratch. In 1929, the year of the Stock Market Crash, his business became highly unstable. He made a few decisions that soured on him, like many businessmen of the time. Anxiety over his interests began to take hold of his life, and before he knew it, he was getting very little sleep. Tranquilizers seemed to provide no relief at all.

So severe was Penney's mental state that he physically contracted shingles, a terribly painful viral disease characterized by skin rashes and blisters. Now his mind and emotions were in shambles, and his body had followed suit. He was hospitalized, and the best doctors did what they could, to no avail. Mind, body, and spirit, J. C. Penney didn't seem long for this world. He believed he had no friends, and that even his family had turned against him.

One dark and dismal night, he somehow convinced himself that his time had come. Before the dawn, he was certain he would depart this life. He began composing a farewell letter to his wife and children. But as the morning light began to shyly peek into his window, he heard a distant melody that made him put his pen down. It was the sound of singing.

The hospital chapel was on the same hall, and the staff members were singing,

Be not dismayed whate'er betide,
God will take care of you;
beneath his wings of love abide,
God will take care of you.

No matter what may be the test,
God will take care of you;
lean, weary one, upon his breast,
God will take care of you.

Why did the sound of distant music accomplish something no doctor could achieve? Penney sat and listened as the words of the hymn seemed to break through the locks and chains on his hopeless soul, and he let the light from heaven inward.

"It's all real," Penney thought. "God loves and cares for me."

That's what he had been taught, and that's what he had always pretended to believe. After all, he descended from a long line of Baptist preachers. Now, however, the love of God was somehow a powerful reality. It had reached deep within him and taken hold of him when nothing else could.

J. C. Penney leaped from his bed with an energy he hadn't felt in months and made his way to the back row of the chapel. He picked up a hymnal and began to sing as the tears rolled down his face. "I can't explain it," he later wrote. "I can only call it a miracle." Afterward, he always said this was the central experience of his entire life.

The revival of his health and his business made for an amazing story. Never again did he allow his life to be hijacked by worry, and it seemed that the more he turned his business over to God, the more it flourished, and the more he gave away to missions and charitable organizations.

My friend, I hope you understand that there is only one master in life who will not enslave you. His name is Jesus Christ, and the only freedom possible is through discovering His love. The way of worry is a twisting road that leads nowhere.

My hope and prayer is that you will turn off that road today and begin walking a new one. Follow Jesus, wherever He may lead you. There is a reason He is known as the Good Shepherd, you see. He will lead you, care for you, and make you to lie down in green pastures, beside still waters. He will restore your soul. And even when you walk through the valley of the shadow, you will fear no evil, because He is with you. This is the way the journey of life was meant to be pursued.

That's the life I intend to live, and the path I intend to follow. My way may not be easy, and the challenges are certain to come. But the destination, we know, is a good one. It is a journey of hope. It is a journey of peace.

Won't you walk with me?

Questions

1. Do you agree or disagree with the statement: "Worry is the assumption that God's wisdom, power, and love aren't big enough for my problem"? Explain your answer.

2. In what ways does the desire to be independent of God fuel our anxieties?

3. Make a list of the concerns you want to put into God's strong and kind hands. What will convince you that He's fully capable of handling them so you don't have to take them back?

4. Why is it important to be aware that you are vulnerable to doubts about God's goodness and purposes in your life?

5. What can you expect as you claim God's promise to care for you, lead you, and provide for you?

6. What is the most significant truth you've learned from this study? Who needs to hear you share it?

Prayer:
Today I choose a new beginning. Forgive me for refusing your comfort and authority. I choose to yield to your best. I trust you to lead me through each challenge. I will rejoice in your faithfulness. Holy Spirit, help me to receive all that God intends. In Jesus' name, amen.

Notes

Notes

Notes

Notes

Using This Book in Classes and Groups

This book is designed for individual study, small groups, and classes. The best way to absorb and apply these principles is for each person to individually study and answer the questions at the end of each chapter, then to discuss them in either a class or a group environment.

Each chapter's questions are designed to promote reflection, application, and discussion. Order enough copies of the book for everyone to have a copy. For couples, encourage both to have their own book so they can record their individual reflections.

A recommended schedule for a small group might be:

Week 1   Introduction to the book. The group leader can tell his own story, share his hopes for the group, and provide books for each person. Encourage people to read the assigned chapter each week and answer the questions.

Weeks 2-6   Each week, introduce the topic for the week and share a story of how God has used the principles in your life. In small groups, lead people through a discussion of the questions at the end of the chapters. In classes, teach the principles in each chapter, use personal illustrations, and invite discussion.

Personalize Each Lesson

Don't feel pressured to cover every question in your group discussions. Pick out three or four that had the biggest impact on you, and focus on those, or ask people in the group to share their responses to the questions that meant the most to them that week.

Make sure you personalize the principles and applications. At least once in each group meeting or class, add your own story to illustrate a particular point.

Make the Scriptures come alive. Far too often, we read the Bible like it's a phone book, with little or no emotion. Paint a vivid picture for people. Provide insights about the context of people's encounters with God, and help people in your class or group sense the emotions of specific people in each scene.

Focus on Application

The questions at the end of each chapter and your encouragement to be authentic will help your group take big steps to apply the principles they're learning. Share how you are applying the principles in particular chapters each week, and encourage them to take steps of growth, too.

Three Types of Questions

If you have led groups for a few years, you already understand the importance of using open questions to stimulate discussion. Three types of questions are *limiting, leading,* and *open*. Many of the questions at the end of each day's lessons are open questions. *Limiting questions* focus on an obvious answer, such as, "What does Jesus call himself in John 10:11?" These don't stimulate reflection or discussion. If you want to use questions like this, follow them with thought-provoking open questions. *Leading questions* sometimes require the listener to guess what the leader has in mind, such as, "Why did Jesus use the metaphor of a shepherd in John 10?" (He was probably alluding to a passage in Ezekiel, but most people wouldn't know that.) The teacher who asks a leading question has a definite answer in mind. Instead of asking this question, he should teach the point and perhaps ask an open question about the point he has made. *Open questions* usually don't have right or wrong answers. They stimulate thinking, and they are far less threatening because the person answering doesn't risk ridicule for being wrong. These questions often begin with "Why do you think…?" or "What are some reasons that…?" or "How would you have felt in that situation?"

About the Author

Allen Jackson has worked with the congregation of World Outreach Church in Murfreesboro, Tennessee since 1981, serving as senior pastor for 22 years.

Under his leadership and vision, the World Outreach Church fellowship has grown from 150 to 10,000. In reaching the local community with the Gospel, the mission seemed clear—help people develop a meaningful relationship with God. Pastor Jackson spearheaded the development of a variety of World Outreach Church community events that provided opportunities for families to experience God, and for some, to become part of a local church. The results have been a stronger community, strengthened families and a healthier church.

Pastor Jackson earned a Bachelor of Arts from Oral Roberts University, a Master of Arts in Religious Studies from Vanderbilt University and studied at Hebrew University in Jerusalem. He has pursued additional studies at Gordon-Conwell Theological Seminary in Boston.

He is an active member of his community, having served on the Board of the American Red Cross and the Community Advisory Board of National Health Corporation Nursing Home. Pastor Jackson chaired the Murfreesboro Area Ministerial Association and was named Outstanding Young Minister by the Jr. Chamber of Commerce. He is a graduate of Leadership Rutherford, a community leadership program developed by the Chamber of Commerce. Jackson was honored as a distinguished community business leader by the Murfreesboro Chamber of Commerce in 2010.

Pastor Jackson has been a featured speaker at a conference conducted by the International Christian Embassy-Jerusalem Feast of Tabernacles celebration in Israel for several years. He has been recognized by the Christian Coalition of the Israeli Knesset for his continued support. Pastor Jackson is a church planter and his passion is to help people, wherever they may be, to become fully devoted followers of Christ. His conviction in serving a God of restoration and effectuating a 24/7 church has touched people across the country and the world. Through Intend Ministries, Jackson coaches pastors across the nation and the world to greater effectiveness in their congregations.

Pastor Jackson is married, and his wife, Kathy, is an active participant in ministry at World Outreach Church.

To Order More Copies

To order more copies of this book
and for discounts for large orders, go to:
www.intendpublishing.com